WEATHER WATCH

A Stormy Day

by Spencer Brinker

Consultant:
Beth Gambro
Reading Specialist
Yorkville, Illinois

Contents

A Stormy Day 2

Key Words 16

Index. 16

About the Author 16

BEARPORT
PUBLISHING

New York, New York

A Stormy Day

Look!
It is stormy.

Today is stormy.

I see a big cloud.

Today is stormy.

I see a rain jacket.

Today is stormy.

I see a huge wave.

Today is stormy.

I see a wet umbrella.

Today is stormy.

I see a deep puddle.

Look around!

What can you see on a stormy day?

Key Words

cloud

jacket

puddle

umbrella

wave

Index

cloud 4–5
jacket 6–7
puddle 12–13
umbrella 10–11
wave 8–9

About the Author

Spencer Brinker lives and works in New York City. Weather never stops him from enjoying the city.

Teaching Tips

Before Reading

✔ Guide readers on a "picture walk" through the text by asking them to name the things shown.

✔ Discuss book structure by showing children where text will appear consistently on pages.

✔ Highlight the supportive pattern of the book. Note the consistent number of sentences and words found on each alternating page.

During Reading

✔ Encourage children to "read with your finger" and point to each word as it is read. Stop periodically to ask readers to point to a specific word in the text.

✔ Reading strategies: When encountering unknown words, prompt readers with encouraging cues, such as:

- **Does that word look like a word you already know?**
- **It could be _____ , but look at _____ .**
- **Check the picture.**

After Reading

✔ Write the key words on index cards.

- **Have readers match them to pictures in the book.**
- **Have children sort words by category (words that end with e, for example).**

✔ Encourage readers to talk about different types of weather.

✔ Ask readers to identify their favorite page in the book. Have them read that page aloud.

✔ Ask children to write their own sentences about the weather. Encourage them to use the same pattern found in the book as a model for their writing.

Credits: Cover, © B Brown/Shutterstock and © MilosVasiljevic/Shutterstock; 2–3, © Craig Zawada/Shutterstock and © phototropic/iStock; 4–5, © TobagoCays/Shutterstock; 6–7, © LukaTBD/iStock; 8–9, © John McCormick/Shutterstock; 10–11, © Niyom Napalai/Shutterstock; 12–13, © Christopher Griffen/Alamy; 14–15, © Pikul Noorod/Shutterstock, and © Dark Moon Pictures/Shutterstock; 16T (L to R), © TobagoCays/Shutterstock and © LukaTBD/iStock; 16B (L to R), © Christopher Griffen/Alamy, © Niyom Napalai/Shutterstock, and © John McCormick/Shutterstock; Back Cover, © Craig Zawada/Shutterstock.

Publisher: Kenn Goin   **Senior Editor:** Joyce Tavolacci   **Creative Director:** Spencer Brinker

Library of Congress Cataloging-in-Publication Data: Names: Brinker, Spencer, author. Title: A stormy day / by Spencer Brinker. Description: New York, New York : Bearport Publishing, [2019] | Series: Weather watch | Audience: Ages 6 to 12. | Includes bibliographical references and index. Identifiers: LCCN 2018015171 (print) | LCCN 2018017693 (ebook) | ISBN 9781642800227 (Ebook) | ISBN 9781642800005 (library) | ISBN 9781642801378 (paperback) Subjects: LCSH: Rain and rainfall—Juvenile literature. | Storms—Juvenile literature. | Weather—Juvenile literature. Classification: LCC QC924.7 (ebook) | LCC QC924.7 .B75 2018 (print) | DDC 551.55—dc23 LC record available at https://lccn.loc.gov/2018015171

Copyright © 2019 Bearport Publishing Company, Inc. All rights reserved. No part of this publication may be reproduced in whole or in part, stored in any retrieval system, or transmitted in any form or by any means, electronic, mechanical, photocopying, recording, or otherwise, without written permission from the publisher. For more information, write to Bearport Publishing Company, Inc., 45 West 21 Street, Suite 3B, New York, New York 10010. Printed in the United States of America.